Workbook

Never Finished

Unshackle Your Mind and
Win the War Within

A Guide to David Goggins' Book

To The Point Publishing

<u>Your Free Gift!</u>

As a thank you for your purchase, we are giving away these best-selling workbooks **for free**!

Scan the QR code below!

IMPORTANT:

This book is a summary and analysis workbook based on Never Finished Unshackle Your Mind and Win the War Within by David Goggins.

This book is meant to enhance your original reading experience, not replace it.

We strongly encourage you to scan the QR code below to purchase the original book.

Disclaimer:

The information provided within this book is for general informational/entertainment purposes only. While we try to keep the information up-to-date and correct, there are no representations or warranties, express or implied, about the completeness, accuracy, reliability, suitability, or availability with respect to the information, products, services, or related graphics contained in this book for any purpose. Any use of this information is at your own risk.

No part of this book may be reproduced or transmitted in any form or by any means, electronic or mechanical, including photocopying, recording or by any information storage and retrieval system, without written permission from the author.

Table of Contents

A Quick Note on How to Use This Workbook

Never Finished is broken down into chapters with an "evolution" that follows each. These evolutions include hard truths and explanations of the lessons learned by David Goggins throughout his life.

This workbook includes a summary of each chapter, the main lesson of each evolution, a summary of each evolution, goals to challenge you, and action steps for you to take in your own life.

The chapters in Never Finished include stories about David's life, how he was able to overcome everything that was thrown his way, and how he became an absolute savage both physically and mentally. The main lessons from each chapter are included above the evolution section and provide a summarized insight into the chapter content.

The goals in each chapter are defined by the chapter content and the lessons in each evolution. To become the savage you want to be and lead the life you want, you need to start making changes, and these goals are the perfect jumping off point.

The action steps in each chapter are also defined by the chapter content and the lessons in the evolution section. These steps are ways in which to implement the lessons learned in this book into your everyday life.

Introduction

There are countless self-help books on the market right now, each promising to "fix" what might be wrong with your life. But, while we may strive to help ourselves or make improvements to our lives, we leave out the most important lesson of all: belief.

In the 1950s, scientist Dr. Curt Richter performed a test on rats that measured the time they would stay swimming in a cylinder full of water. In the first test, he found that the rats would swim for no more than fifteen minutes before giving up; some giving up sooner than others. In the second test, right before it appeared the rat would give up, Richter would pick it up, dry it off, let it rest, and then put it back into the cylinder. This time, the rats would swim for an average of sixty hours without any food or rest.

So, what did this test represent? Belief.

The second batch of rats believed that they would be saved, so they kept swimming for hours and hours. They refused to give up.

There are two levels to belief: one being surface level and the other being belief born in resilience. Surface level belief is the one we are all most familiar with. Our parents and teachers tell us to always "believe in yourself," but that only goes so deep. The belief that is born through resilience is what keeps us swimming for hours even when our bodies want to give up.

Resilience is created from working through pain and ignoring the temptation to quit. It makes you certain of your strengths and eliminates doubt. But resilience doesn't come from someone else; it comes from within. It is built through struggle and empowers the belief that keeps you moving forward on the hardest days.

The problem is that while most people feel they are missing something in their lives, they aren't willing to make the changes to go after it. Their belief isn't strong enough to bring that grit and resiliency to the surface to kick them in the ass to get going and to keep going. Even if they start, they find themselves walking back on their belief at the first sign of resistance, and then later feeling that familiar sense of unfulfillment.

Social media and modern dialogue around self-improvement only hinder this process further. We are too focused on wishing for something different—a head start or better looks or more money—that we get stuck where we are, envious of something that didn't happen.

These roadblocks that keep us from reaching our full potential and maximizing it are all inside our heads. We choose to live this way, but we can change our way of being and thinking to regain control of our lives.

The work is hard, but through that struggle, resilience is built. With that resilience comes a deep belief in ourselves and our capabilities.

This book is a bootcamp for your brain. Changing how you think will change how you live your life. Rewiring your mind and heart will help you realize your inner strengths and maximize your potential.

Chapter 1: Maximize Minimal Potential

In 2018, David Goggins received the Veterans of Foreign Wars (VFW) prestigious Americanism Award at a convention in Kansas City. Other veterans such as John McCain had received the same award for their service to their country. Before being called up to accept the reward and give a speech, David found himself stuck thinking about his life.

David was born a loser. He didn't grow up in a good home. He wasn't given opportunities, but still he was receiving the award. In that moment, he didn't feel worthy of the award.

As his name was called and he walked up to the stage, he thought about what the catalyst was for his transformation from loser to winner. How had he gone from a 300-pound exterminator at 24 years old to the Navy SEAL receiving the same award given to John McCain?

David choked up when he went to speak, and as he began to thank his mother, he completely broke down. It hit him in that moment that his life had changed when he went to visit his father for the last time.

At 24-years old, David was broken. Working a dead-end job, quitting on his goals when things got hard, and going numb to absolutely everything around him, he was a loser.

Born to a father who often abused him, his mother, and his brother, David had grown up blaming all his problems on the circumstances around him. He was born a loser whose goal was survival rather than learning to thrive, and surviving meant living a miserable life.

To finally find something to pull him out of his misery, he went to see his father in Buffalo, New York.

When David was eight, his mother had packed up the family and left her abusive husband to move to Indiana. Growing up away from his father, David wondered if everything he had experienced as a kid, and the experiences of his mother, were true. He needed to confront his past.

On the drive to visit his father, David found himself thinking that his life and how it had turned out wasn't his fault; it was the best he could do with what he had been given. But he also asked himself, how long will I let my past define my future?

When he finally arrived, his father greeted him warmly and affectionately. They caught up, laughed, and went to the bar his father ran—just like old times. As he sat in the office, waiting for his father to finish spinning records upstairs, he was appalled by how much his father's life had not changed. Everything was the same, despite the years. Even the dirty old couch hadn't been updated.

For years, David had pictured his father as the Devil, but he now saw him for who he truly was: just a man.

After the night was over, his father was sloppy drunk and no longer the affectionate man he had been earlier. Sitting in at a Denny's, David's father began saying horrible things about his ex-wife and her parents. When David asked him to stop, he grew angry, but so did David. The fire in David's eyes put his father in check quickly, turning him into a frightened old man who no longer wielded any power over his son.

That was it the whole time, David realized. His father held power over people by beating them down physically and verbally, but the minute someone took it away, he was weak. David wanted to claim his father was the reason for his life being so pathetic up until that point, but that would just give him more power. He was ready to take back his own life and break the cycle.

After being a prisoner stuck in his own mind for years, David finally broke free and began his evolution into the person worthy of the Americanism Award.

Savage lessons

1. Even if you're born a loser, that doesn't mean you have to live your life that way forever.
2. No one is going to change your life but you.
3. You give people power over you. Take it back.

Evolution No. 1

The lesson: Distractions weigh you down. Shift your focus and move forward.

Everyone has suffered in some way, shape or form in their life. It is easy to get distracted by how these events hold you back or stunt your growth, instead of learning to accept them and move forward.

Becoming mentally trapped by the fear of letting go comes from not knowing what the future may hold. So many people get stuck in this fog that leaves them weak and lazy instead of using it to fuel their desire for change. No one is going to come along and change your life for you; it is all up to you. Letting go of your past and focusing on making the future what you want will propel you forward.

Goals

1. Write down one excuse you consistently use when you don't reach a goal.
2. Write down two events that happened in your past that are still present in your mind on a regular basis.

Action Steps

Next time you find yourself leaning on an excuse based on a past trauma, take a moment to reflect. Ask yourself, is this really impacting my life or am I allowing it to?

Next time you find yourself afraid to step forward or go after a goal that you want, confront what is making you afraid. Whether that is a person who caused you harm or an internal thought about your self-worth, confront it head on and ask yourself if this is really who you want to be.

Chapter 2: Merry Fucking Christmas

For most people, Christmas is a time of year for family and giving, but for David, it has always been just another day. In 2018, him and his wife met up for breakfast with his brother and mother. While they had all shared the similar experience of dealing with their father's abuse, they all chose to react differently, and David realized that choice set them all apart.

For his brother, who had always tried to be a peacekeeper and had run to his room when their father hit their mother, he denied that anything had happened. He still regularly visited their father and went to Buffalo for Christmas to see his grave. Denial filled his past and allowed him to live with a fictionalized childhood.

For his mother, she chose to avoid the pain and memories until she had none left. She went with David's brother to visit Buffalo and see the old home, but she said she didn't recognize any of it. Trauma can cause people to have serious memory loss if they choose to push it to the back of their mind and not confront it. As you forget the painful memories, others from the same time slip away as well.

David did not go with his family to Buffalo. Instead him and his wife were planning to visit her family in Florida. As they waited before their flight, his recently published book *Can't Hurt Me*, hit the New York Times Bestseller List.

The publication of this book was a huge milestone for David. After being repeatedly turned down, told that his story wasn't one people wanted to hear, and that they couldn't relate to his struggles, he finally secured a publisher and a large check. But, when he thought about someone else holding publishing rights to his story, he didn't like it.

So, he gave back the money, cut ties, and published the book as an independent. No one thought he would find success as a first-time author, but his wife was there to help him. Independently publishing was just one more roadblock he knew he could overcome after a life of struggle.

As they relished in the fact that the book was a bestseller, David felt his heart beat out of rhythm. As a trained EMT with years of experience, he knew he was in A-fib. After hours of trying to get his heart beating correctly using techniques he frequently used as an EMT, he knew it was time to go to the hospital.

Instead of getting on a plane to Florida, him and his wife went to the ER. Doctors told him they would need to shock his heart to get it beating normally again. While waiting, David found time to reflect on his life.

With two heart surgeries under his belt, he hadn't been afraid to die in the past, but with the recent success of his published story, he wasn't ready to go. He was given space to speak and share his truth with the world and was already speaking and teaching others to live a resilient life based on the lessons he'd learned. But that's life.

David's heart began beating normally again after the successful shock and he was able to go home. Life throws us curveballs all the time and it is up to us to get back up and not stay knocked down. That is what "Merry Fucking Christmas," is all about—those unexpected gifts that life throws at you.

Savage lessons

1. Sometimes life tosses you curveballs; it is up to you how you want to view and learn from them.
2. People handle trauma in different ways. Your experiences don't define you—how you grow past them defines you.
3. Success comes when you pursue your passion, your way.

Evolution No. 2

The lesson: Never waste anything. Use your fear, hate, and the hate from others to fuel your rise.

Never let anything go to waste. Whether that is eating all your food, using all your toothpaste, or mining the hatred thrown your way on the internet, don't let anything go to waste.

David created an incredible way to utilize your fears and hate to fuel your climb. When training for a bike race across America, he found himself afraid of riding for days on end without sleep, with only the road for company. Instead of letting the fear control him, he took out a recorder and spoke aloud all his fears, then listened to it back.

Listening to your fears can help you realize just how minimal they really are. Everything in your head always seems bigger than it actually is, but by listening to yourself over and over discuss your feelings and fears, they become less of a nightmare.

Each day, we talk to ourselves and listen to that voice inside our heads that tells us to get out of bed or makes an excuse for us not to workout. If we choose instead to speak that voice out loud, we will hear how weak our excuses are. Change the fear, hate, and excuses into optimism and empowerment that fuels you to keep moving up.

David uses this same technique to combat haters online. He records himself reading their hateful comments and listens to it on a regular basis. There is more fuel to stoke your inner fire in hate. Don't let people back you into a small corner with their words; let them fuel your passion to prove them wrong and show them what you can do.

Goals

1. Describe a time where someone gave you a negative comment, either online or in person. Write this down and place it somewhere you can see it each day to remind yourself of what is fueling your fire.
2. Write down a time where you got a "Merry Fucking Christmas" present thrown at you from life.

Action Steps

Next time you find yourself listening to the voice inside your head, whether it is giving you an excuse or telling you to be afraid, take out a recorder and record your thoughts. Listen to your thoughts back. Do you feel the same?

Next time someone says something negative to or about you, store the comment away on a piece of paper. Put that paper somewhere you can see it and let it fuel your desire to reach a new goal.

Chapter 3: The Mental Lab

Following the release of *Can't Hurt Me*, David found success and a spotlight. For years, he had always worked in the shadows, grinding away at the gym or studying late into the night while others were out partying. But now that he was being watched, he felt the weight of it all and knew that he couldn't fall back into any old habits. He had to continue practicing what he preached and moving forward.

After his visit with his father at 24, David became fascinated with the power of the mind and how positive or negative thoughts could work for or against us. Learning how to harness and channel the emotions and situational conditions our minds constantly find themselves in eventually allowed David to accomplish things he never thought possible. He dubbed this process the building of a Mental Lab.

David's Mental Lab building started after he visited his father. He realized his life gave him all the raw materials needed to transform himself. Working out and hitting the books, he pushed himself to prepare for Navy SEAL training and testing. He knew that the root problems he faced in training were all mental, and he needed to change himself inside.

The shift in David's mindset meant he built himself a strong Mental Lab where his savage self was Goggins and the scared boy was David. He experimented by letting the physical workouts become mental workouts by seeing how long his mental fortitude would last as he applied more pressure. Throughout this process, the alter-ego Goggins became a complete savage who refused to quit under pressure.

Using a Mental Lab, you can transform yourself into the person you want to be. Experimenting and locking yourself in can help you hone the attitudes and reactions you need to have to live the life you want. Unfortunately for David, following his Christmas health scare, he found himself locked outside of his Mental Lab.

At this time, he received an email asking if he would participate in running the Leadville Trail 100 to raise money for charity. After running multiple 100-milers in previous years, this shouldn't have been a difficult decision, but it was. David was worried if he would be able to physically compete due to his heart issues and being out of shape. He realized this back and forth in his mind was him being locked out of his Mental Lab and away from the savage Goggins.

In the time following his book's success, he had grown complacent. Sure, he still worked out twice a day, but he wasn't the savage—physically or mentally—that he had been. It was a wake-up call for him. Not only did he realize that his mental resilience faded if not used consistently, but also that he had let his savage self be locked up.

He put together a training plan and agreed to participate in the race. To prepare for the race in the mountains, he trained during the hot summer months along the east coast. He ran 100 miles every week, no excuses. Even on the hottest day of the year, he was out there running. When someone stopped and asked why, he told them candidly "because you're not." He was back to that savage who didn't come in second.

Savage lessons

1. Your thoughts are in control—be aware of how you choose to think.
2. Create a mental lab to give yourself a place to create the savage you want to be.
3. Resilience takes consistent practice. Every day you have the choice to push forward or be complacent.

Evolution No. 3

The lesson: Just one second can change the outcome of your life.

There are a finite number of seconds in each day. No matter what struggles you are going through, at some point, they will come to an end. But in those single seconds are also opportunities to quit or to keep going.

When David was in Hell Week during Navy SEAL training, he found himself having a moment where he didn't think he wanted to be a SEAL anymore. He wanted to get out of the frightening ocean, a hot shower, and to give up, but he didn't. It is in these moments where we make self-sabotaging impulsive and emotional decisions.

Instead of letting impulse win, he practiced "taking a knee," which was controlling his breathing and anxiety enough to think clearly about his decision. It was a single-second decision to breathe instead of quitting, and that made all the difference. Each day we battle the single seconds that determine whether we give up or keep going. Winning these seconds repeatedly is what moves us forward.

These split-second decisions are made easier by having a purpose or baseline. For David, he knew he wanted to be a SEAL. That meant he couldn't give up if he was going to live the fulfilling life he wanted. In that case, the decision to keep going was easier. Not easy, but easier.

Waking up and challenging yourself to embrace the struggle and grow resilient is what will lead you to a more fulfilling life.

Goals

1. Describe honestly who your alter-ego residing in your Mental Lab is. Are they who you want them to be?
2. Write down your purpose or baseline for a goal you're working toward. Put the note somewhere you can see it when you need to make that single-second decision.

Action Steps

Next time you find yourself in a situation where you are struggling with a decision due to a lack of confidence in who you are, create a person who would say "yes." What do they look like? How do they think? Become that person.

Next time you find yourself in a situation where your anxiety is spiking and you feel like quitting whatever you're doing, take a knee.

Chapter 4: A Savage Reborn

Two weeks before the Leadville race, David and his wife arrived in Colorado to begin training and acclimatizing to the altitude. As he trained though, David found himself struggling with his pace. His body was ready to give up, but he found his mind hardening back into that savage he had been before.

David knew that he needed to do the race, even if he had to walk the whole 100 miles. His mind was where it needed to be. The savage inside was prepared and was craving the worst conditions because it knew that would bring out the pressure to make him do his best.

It is this pressure that turns people into savages, and that is what David was ready for. He studied the course, the mountains, and the flat sections where he could run faster. He also studied the false summits, where you think you are almost done but then find one more climb left. These are just like what happens in life, when you think you've reached the end only to find one more hill, set, or task. It's the struggle through the journey that changes you as a person and teaches you to focus on what is happening instead of looking for the end.

Running a 100-mile race brings a lot of buried thoughts to the surface. It makes you reflect on who you are and what made you that way. While running, David found himself reflecting on the stutter he developed in the third grade. It may have been due to his past trauma, but he felt exposed and did everything he could to get out of reading aloud or even participating in class. Every morning and night, he thought about how stupid and worthless he was, which only fueled his stutter more.

This is exactly what many people struggle with daily. Perhaps it's not a stutter, but something else. They wake up and go to bed thinking about not being good enough or not being a certain way and using it as an excuse or shortcut in life. They use it as a way to tap out before they can become extraordinary.

Now, running in one of the most difficult races on earth, David found strength in his past weakness. He had overcome the stutter and had pushed himself to accomplish so much. He wasn't about to give up now.

As he got closer to the finish line, David's pacer started to fall behind. Instead of leaving him, David decided to turn around to help him. As they walked together, a man passed and stopped to tell David that his son had challenged him to catch David.

This comment threw David out of balance. When he was a full-time savage before, he never let a comment slide off; he felt challenged to rise and prove them wrong. He was a savage beast, unbalanced, but obsessed with being hungry. And he had let that beast be tamed over the past few years. But that one comment brought the beast back out.

He ran hard and caught up with the guy, passing him to beat him to the finish line, all the while being led by his north star: being the hardest motherfucker ever.

After finishing, he was changed. What more could he do now as a savage at forty-five?

Savage lessons

1. Pressure creates savagery. Being a savage means staying hungry.
2. Focus on the present instead of when you can finally quit.
3. Let the doubters and haters fuel your fire. Anger can be a potent gasoline.

Evolution No. 4

The lesson: Have the courage to make a Hard Stop when you find yourself losing your soul.

David's mother suffered greatly at the hands of his father, and while she did eventually leave to live a better life, she never rebuilt herself the way David did. Instead, she took the creativity that comes after destruction, and built herself new walls to keep people out.

While she seemed to be successful on the outside, she saw herself as worthless and undeserving on the inside because that is what David's father had taught her she was. She hustled because she couldn't stand to be alone with her own thoughts. She tried to help others because she couldn't save herself.

David's father was charming to her when they first met, but with every strike and negative comment, he chipped away her bright soul. This didn't happen overnight, but with time, she became a shell of who she was. And after leaving, she could never rebuild herself properly.

David describes a Hard Stop as a full stop on pushing forward, giving yourself time to reconsider with a clear mind and take stock of where you are at. If you take a hard look at what is happening around you, you can see things more clearly and choose a different path forward.

While it may take great strength to leave certain situations, David knows that sometimes all it takes is to get angry. Not irrational rage, but controlled anger that wakes you up and gives you the energy and bravery to change your situation. Anger is a powerful tool that can destroy the walls around you and leave room in the destruction for new creation.

Goals

1. Write down your first thoughts when you wake up and when you go to bed. Are they self-deprecating? What can you do to change them?
2. Write "Hard Stop" on a notecard and leave it somewhere you can grab when needed. By taking a physical Hard Stop, you can slow down your mind to think clearly about whether you have started down a path that will lead to an avalanche.

Action Steps

Think critically about a time when someone made a comment to you that threw gasoline on your fire. Just like the runner's comment to David that pushed him to finish, what did this comment do to you? How can you harness that same fire in your everyday life?

Next time you find yourself heading down a path you know isn't right or when you find someone is stealing your soul, get angry. Use the controlled anger to make you brave enough to change the situation.

Chapter 5: Disciple of Discipline

Following the 100-mile run at Leadville, David found himself curled up on the floor of his room, his body shaking and his bowels emptying. This was typical after such a physical exertion, so he knew what to expect. But it was the mental release that was about to happen that would change him.

As he lay there in agony, his mind filtered back to when he was a child. After leaving his father, his mother took them to their grandparent's house in Indiana. It was here that he got to know his grandfather, Sgt. Jack, a WWII veteran and rigid disciplinarian.

That first morning, David and his brother were woken up at dawn and given a task list of chores to do. Every single day started like this and ended with another task list. Whether it was mowing, picking up leaves, sweeping the porches, or clearing snow, David always had a list. Not long after realizing he'd have to do chores each day, David's brother moved back to Buffalo with their father. But David stayed.

As he grew up, David learned that these chores were there to teach him discipline and other valuable lessons. Eventually, he changed from the scared kid who didn't understand why his grandfather would treat him so terribly into someone who appreciated and took pride in the work he did. Not only did it please his grandfather, but seeing a job well done made him happy as well. A half-assed job isn't the way you want to live your life, and David realized that quickly.

So many people rely on excuses or half-assed jobs to get them through life and then sit wondering why they feel so bad. No one is going to do the work for you, if you want your life to be different, you need to become a disciple of discipline. Find that sense of pride in the work you do and do it without fail.

When David was a teenager, him and his mother moved into an apartment, and he found himself failing school. He needed to graduate if he was ever to follow his dream and join the Air Force, so he moved back in with his grandparents. He went right back to the task lists his grandfather gave him and jumped back into a life of discipline.

No one is born with everything; everyone has something they are missing or disadvantaged by. The difference between those who find success and those who wallow is discipline. Maximizing what you do have and using discipline to increase your workload, your output will double or triple.

Becoming a disciple of discipline will instill in you the drive to keep pushing, to keep striving to be better and do better than you thought you could. It was the lessons learned from Sgt. Jack that kept David going and taught him the discipline needed to become the man he was meant to be.

Savage lessons

1. Discipline makes you consistent. Consistency makes you savage.
2. Letting fear control you only holds you back.
3. Everyone has some sort of disadvantage. You are not special.

Evolution No. 5

The lesson: Self-pity makes you weak. It is through humility that we learn just what we are capable of accomplishing.

Pity can quickly turn toxic. No one besides maybe close friends or family actually care about your struggles. If you sit and grumble about your situation, it may bring you comfort at that moment, but it quickly turns into an excuse for not changing your life. Pity steals your inner strength and self-esteem and can lead you down a road to depression.

The only thing that truly matters is the present. If you wallow in pity or depression, it steals your time that could be spent doing something more productive. When David lived with Sgt. Jack, there was no pity given despite the horrible circumstances he had lived through. The chores needed done, no matter what. David didn't have time to feel sorry for himself, and he quickly learned no one else cared about his problems.

Humility combats self-pity. Whether you are humbled by the fact that everyone works a shitty job at first or by the fact that everyone struggles in life, it pushes away the pity and helps you focus on the moment.

Training yourself to shed the entitlement and instead focus on learning and growing from the bottom up will make you hungrier to learn more and keep pushing you forward. Trained humility is service to others and strength within yourself.

Goals

1. Create a task list for yourself each morning to get done before starting your day. This could include making the bed or doing dishes, but it should always get done.
2. Work or volunteer at least one day each week doing a job that is humble. Whether it is picking up trash, flipping burgers, or helping others, humble yourself by doing something from the bottom.

Action Steps

Next time you find yourself thinking "this is beneath me," take a moment to humble yourself. Write down at least one lesson you learn that day by performing the task or job that you think is "beneath you."

Create a plan that will turn you into a disciple of discipline. Make task lists, set alarms, let go of self-pity, and get moving.

Chapter 6: The Art of Getting Hit in the Mouth

The 100-mile race had reminded David that he wanted more and always had strived for more. Jumping back in also meant he saw the sport had become more popular and accessible. This made him question what the new deep end was. What was the next thing he could do that would be an immense challenge?

Each race pushes you further, making you rewire your brain to tell it, "Yes, I can do this." When David was learning to swim as a teenager, he realized that the mind needed to be tricked because it held you back so much. Even when he was a proficient swimmer, he always stuck to the shallow end because it was safe. When that fear sits in the back of your mind, taunting you, that means it's time to re-evaluate.

Being afraid isn't bad; it's a good motivator to let us know when we have become too comfortable and when it's time to push forward again. We fear the unknown even when we have outgrown the known.

In search of the next deep end, David found a 240-mile race in the Moab desert in Nevada. Feeling mentally and physically prepared, despite the fear of doing something completely new, David showed up ready to run the race.

The course was completely different, with mountains, rough terrain, and stretches of desert. It was during a stretch of the desert that David found himself struggling, not because of the heat but because of the cold. In October, the wind whipped across the terrain and chilled him. David suffers from Raynaud's phenomenon, meaning the blood flow is restricted to his extremities in cold weather. This meant that as he ran through the cold desert, his hands and feet became nearly unusable. Unable to even open his pack to grab water, he jogged to the aid station and had to have one of his crew members put heated gloves on his hands for him.

With his hands warmed up, David set back out and continued eating miles with his pacers.

Throughout the race, David knew how important situational awareness was, not just to maintain footing on the harsh terrain but also to make sure he didn't run off course being out in the middle of nowhere. As he found his stride and zoned out, he trusted his pacer to watch the GPS and keep them on course. But, instead of checking in and using situational awareness, they both got far off track.

When the pacer's phone finally got service again, he noticed dozens of missed calls and texts from the organizers who had been tracking them and saw they were off course. David wasn't mad though; he knew it was his fault for not checking in and letting his situational awareness wane. You can't let someone else lead you in your own race.

Directing blame toward others instead of recognizing the problems stemmed from you doesn't solve anything. Accepting your mistakes and moving on allows you to deal with the problems faster and with a clearer head.

Another problem quickly came up for David as he was about halfway through the race. He needed to take his medication for his thyroid and rest. Unfortunately, this meant his body thought the race was over and his muscles began to tighten up. After resting for 12 hours, he was back out on the course but this time with legs feeling like stones and in eightieth place. He felt the pull toward giving up, making excuses that his body had always been sickly, but he knew that wasn't an option.

Picking yourself up after getting knocked down is incredibly hard, which is why you need to learn to absorb the punch without falling. Tough times lead to opportunities for exponential growth. Cultivating this willingness to succeed will push you through those tough times and help you grow.

As the race carried on, David found himself struggling to breathe. He told his issues to his pacer, sounding the whole time like he was trying to find an excuse to quit. He kept going. When he finally thought the issues were too bad to continue, the only option was to walk to the next checkpoint. He kept going. It only takes one step to take the next. But when a medical team arrived to meet him on the trail, David made the decision to leave for a hospital.

He had high-altitude pulmonary edema, meaning there was fluid in his lungs. After spending a few hours in the hospital getting fixed, he was discharged; however, the race had already labeled him as a DNF (did not finish). Instead of accepting that, he rested, got up, and kept running.

While he didn't feel worthy to cross the finish line since he had been DNF'd, he still felt inspired to reach the end and knew what needed to be done differently to race again the following year.

Savage lessons

1. Always search for that next thing that will push you closer to becoming the person you want to be.
2. Blaming someone else for your mistakes only leads you down a spiraling negative path where nothing gets solved.
3. Use what you learn when you fail to fuel your next attempt.

Evolution No. 6

The lesson: If you don't have people in your foxhole who will push you, get them out of there.

The people you surround yourself with can make all the difference in the world. If they don't understand and push you, then they aren't the right people. David describes this as the foxhole, which is a fighting position where you are surrounded with the people who are willing to fight next to you.

The way you find the people who you want in your foxhole is through intentionality, but you also need to know who you are first.

David struggled to figure out who he was after leaving the Air Force at 24-years old. He knew he wanted to be a hard motherfucker but didn't know how to do that. That was when a care package arrived, he saw a documentary about Navy SEALs and knew that was his dream.

As he started to pursue this dream though, he found people around him began questioning what he was doing and were resistant to the change. David realized that as he evolved, his foxhole needed to as well.

After receiving the VFW award, David realized he wasn't ready for retirement and decided to get into wildland firefighting. His wife supported him completely and would block off that time of year for him so he could devote time and focus to being the best firefighter. She is in his foxhole because of her devotion not just to him, but to his goals. Similarly, he is devoted to her and her goals. When she mentioned wanting to run a marathon, he trained with her and pushed her. It is these types of people you want in your foxhole.

Goals

1. Make a list of the people who are currently in your foxhole. What qualities do they have that make them good foxhole companions?
2. Make a list of things that you need to stay aware of for situational awareness. These could be related to work projects or house projects or personal goals. Make a list for at least 1 project or goal.

Action Steps

Next time you must quit something, whether that is a race or a project or a goal, take time to assess how you can try again and get further the next time.

Interview the people who are currently in your foxhole and ask them how they are willing to push you to accomplish your goals and dreams.

Chapter 7: The Reckoning

Following the race in Moab, David got home and immediately was up the next morning running and training for the race the following year. Unfortunately, after a few months of training, his knee began to swell and cause a lot of pain. After an MRI, David knew his knee was messed up.

A few weeks before heading off to fire training, he visited a specialist doctor who worked every day on his knee to get it back into working order. Despite getting through the fire season, a slip at the very end left David with a dislocated knee and doctors telling him to take a few months off.

While this news was bad, David didn't let it affect him. A bad attitude can quickly spiral out of control and infect your life. He knew staying positive was how he would keep himself going. Everyone gets knocked down, but it's up to you how you decide to get up. For David, discipline got him up and that fire was set again to push him to overcome the setback.

He set the goal to still run the Moab race and began strategizing how to get there. David always sets goals that are not easy to reach; they force him to step up and push himself in ways he never thought were possible. Setting goals that stretch your limits push you further along the line and set you up for greater success in the future.

Learning to go to bed in the net positive, making sure to get things done instead of letting a hard day set you back from your goals, will help you stay dedicated to the growth you want in your life. It was during this rehabilitation time for David that the 2020 COVID-19 virus first hit, and everything was shut down. Just like his knee, he realized that our society was fragile. But everyone was suffering. Instead of feeling lost, David was mentally prepared to handle the ups and downs that came with the new world.

With the mindset that everyone struggles, and it is your choices that define who you are and what you can do, David continued his training. While he had a lot of help from his physical therapist, he knew that the only person who could make the difference was him. If you only practice or study when you have to, you'll never get better. David knew this from struggling so much in school as a kid, so he put his mind to getting better.

David ran the Moab race, and was feeling great too, until the tendon in his foot swelled up and forced him to stop. Calling in his physical therapist, he was able to endure the pain of a quick fix. In fact, he laughed through it and felt that hunger grow as he used the pain as fuel for his fire.

When David approached the same section of Moab where he had to stop the year prior and be taken to the hospital, he was afraid. But facing your fears head-on creates the space and sows the seeds for growth. By consistently facing your fears, you gain confidence and learn to master that fear to discover unlimited possibilities.

David finished the race in second place after all kinds of injuries in the second half. His mind knew what he wanted, and it pushed him to get it.

Following the Moab race, David signed up to run across Florida in a 200-mile race no one had yet completed. He completed it and found himself to be in the best shape of his life at forty-five years old. Both physically and mentally, he was a savage.

But after so many years of running, David's knee needed fixed. After debating, he decided to have surgery on his knees to cut away some of the tissue that was causing problems. While he should have recovered and been back to training in 2 weeks, he found himself in a mountain of pain and barely able to walk.

Savage lessons

1. A bad attitude can quickly spiral you out of control.
2. Setting a goal isn't enough; it has to push you past where you think your limits are.
3. Face your fears head on. No exceptions.

Evolution No. 7

The lesson: There is always a standard—be the one who sets your own standard.

Real leadership isn't just about who is at the top, making the most money, and calling the shots. David discovered the power of true leadership while in the Tactical Air Control Party unit.

While there, David was selected for Air Assault School: a brutal 10-day program designed to be a true test that half the class would fail. He chose not to study or train in his spare time, even though he knew he could be called to the program at any time. When it was finally his turn, he met a captain in his class who blew everyone else out of the water. While David and his classmates were content to do what was the requirement, this captain went above and did more. He wasn't there just to pass, but to push himself and grow.

While most people rely on bosses or coaches to give us the motivation to keep going, this captain had internal motivation to smash every single standard the school had set up. And this made him the one to follow, not because he spoke a single word but because he embodied what leadership meant by acting like a leader and doing the work.

The entire class wanted to be like him, beat him, and compete with him. He raised everyone up with him by exposing their lack of dedication.

Learning to self-lead is preparing yourself for what you want in life. While David went into the school winging-it, the captain had prepared and knew exactly what he wanted to accomplish. We can all prepare and self-lead every day to accomplish the goals we set for ourselves.

Goals

   1. Sign up or participate in one activity that is an intense challenge for you. Whether it be running a marathon, writing a book, or building something, do it and push yourself to not give up when it gets tough.
   2. Write an oath that you can follow, that embodies yourself, and sets the stage for who

you want to be. Hang it somewhere you will see it every day.

Action Steps

Next time you find yourself setting a goal, push it a little bit farther. Take that little extra step to show yourself that you can do more.

Find one part of your life where there is a standard that everyone around you follows. Whether it be at the gym, school, or work, find one standard and set your own instead. Go beyond to find fulfillment and drive within yourself.

Chapter 8: Play Until the Whistle

After knee surgery, David could barely move. What should have taken him hours to recover from, had obviously not gone correctly. After weeks of suffering in pain, the doctor finally revealed that he had done some additional surgery without David's knowledge. While he may have had good intentions, it was obviously a bad decision.

After struggling to recover, David came to the realization that he would likely never be back to running like he was prior to the surgery. This meant that a core piece of him, ever since he was 24 and had decided to get in shape to be a SEAL, was gone.

It was during these months that David and his wife searched for answers until finally finding a doctor who could do meniscus replacement surgery. It was the chance David was looking for to be able to get back to his old life and pursue his dream of being a smokejumper: a firefighter who parachuted into the backwoods to put out fires right away.

While David was told he wasn't a fit for meniscus replacement surgery, the doctor did suggest another procedure that would put a plate into his knee. If it was a success, he would eventually make a full recovery, back to his athletic level before. David didn't pass up the opportunity.

After the surgery, he had to take it slow and didn't know if he would ever be able to do what he had prior.

Every day, people struggle and fight against things that happen to them. There are new situations that mean you have to rethink what your 100 percent is and find new ways to give it. This was no different for David, and he wasn't just anyone—he was a savage.

Since he couldn't run, especially not right away after the surgery, David went back to cycling. He pushed himself to try and prepare for a cycling race a few months out. Making it a physical and mental priority to keep pushing himself.

At the start of the race, he was nervous about riding a bike in the outdoors since all his training had been done indoors. In the middle of the race, he stopped. The pain in his knee was too much for him to bear. But he was a savage motherfucker, and he wasn't about to quit. David finished in second place after being off crutches for only seven weeks.

After recovering physically, David kept pushing himself, even running through the pain for the 4x4x48 charity event. Although he wanted to become a smokejumper, he knew the doctor said parachuting was the one thing he couldn't do on his new knee. So, he took up his time with other things, like physical activity and working at a hospital, where he was doing everything from setting up IVs to cleaning poop.

Being a savage doesn't just mean pushing when things are hard; it also means taking the time to adjust your plans to reach new goals. When David couldn't run the 4x4x48 in 2021 after surgery, he did circuit workouts instead. When he had down time during his surgery recovery, he took an EMT class and got further certifications. Moving forward and making progress takes time and it's the lessons learned along the way that are the most important.

Savage lessons

1. You choose whether you give up or keep going. So keep going.
2. If you can't tackle your goal the way you thought originally, choose a new way. Make it happen.
3. When you find yourself sitting idle, choose something new to help you continue your growth.

Evolution No. 8

The lesson: Everyone can be great, but achieving greatness takes hard work and dedication.

Greatness is possible for everyone to achieve if they are willing to go for it. You have everything you need to let go of your faults and pull together all your energy to excel at what you set your mind to.

David sees the line between atmosphere and space the same way that he sees the glimmer of greatness that runs through everyone's soul. Reaching that line only takes the willingness to extend yourself to it. Whether you reach it or not, success is just another milestone along the journey.

Everyone comes with a story of why they can't achieve greatness, but they are just that, stories we make up for ourselves to feel better about our decisions and failures. This identity we craft for ourselves just leaves us trapped instead of freeing us. It is only through evolving and developing new skills that we can move forward and achieve that greatness for ourselves.

Self-exploration leads to greatness but comes about through dedication and hunger for something other than what you've been given. The real work steps in when you start that exploration and break free of the identity that is holding you back.

Goals

1. Write down what your current identity is, then write down all the ways that it is currently holding you back from being who you want to be.
2. Write down one alternative way that you can accomplish a goal or finish a project. Sit and think about new and creative ways that you can tackle life and the curveballs it throws at you.

Action Steps

Next time you find yourself thinking about why you can't do something based on how you were raised or how you are viewed by others, take a knee and ask yourself whether this identity is self-inflicted and holding you back from reaching your potential.

When you feel yourself taking time off, find one new thing to do that is interesting or fun. It doesn't have to require a lot of effort or work but find one way to continue learning and growing.

Chapter 9: Wringing Out the Soul

Despite warnings from his doctor about avoiding parachuting, David decided to enlist in smokejumper school. But this wasn't jump school wasn't just anywhere, it was in freezing British Columbia, where the parachutes didn't let you land easy. They brought you down fast and hard into the snow.

As the oldest in the class, David knew he had competition, and the youngsters were coming after him to prove they were better. But David had done this dance before, and he was up early every day to run in the freezing terrain to keep training. He was a willing warrior, and they don't reach for excuses, ever.

He didn't need to be here training; he was retired, and he didn't need the money or the mental or physical training. But this is where he chose to be. He wanted to do this.

During training, he ran with the younger students and was only 15 seconds slower than his person best in the mile-and-a-half sprint. He also kept to the front of the pack when training in the elements and running distance. The young students inspired David to push himself and help push them.

Smokejumper training was different than SEAL training in that David found he didn't get the same feeling when he saw someone freeze up with fear. As a SEAL, he was immature and felt elevated when he could do something someone else couldn't. But that wasn't a good leader, and in smokejumper training, he needed to be a leader for the team.

Even David struggled during training with tying knots in the cold with his fingers growing too stiff to even move because of his Raynaud's. Despite this struggle, he never hung his head in defeat because he wasn't going to accept defeat. If you think you've been defeated, you already are. David practiced over and over outside in the cold until he was able to tie the knots and cut down on his test time.

The entire process of training and smokejumper school changed David. He realized that you don't have to be the best at everything; being a great person and leader means that you kept pushing in the face of long odds.

After graduating from training, David made his first jump, and his leg didn't break. Together, as a class, everyone made their jumps, and with more practice, got even better. At graduation, David knew this was the place he was meant to be with the people he was meant to be with.

The surgery had been only 10 and a half months prior and here he was, a certified smokejumper. But that wasn't the end. David was already looking ahead to that next challenge.

The road to success isn't a straight line, and David knows that best. It doesn't matter where you come from. Everyone is hindered in some way, but it's how you choose to continue the fight every day that makes you a savage. Even after reaching the goal you set for yourself, it's time to push further and reach for another goal that will force you to grow even more.

You don't have to be like David and run hundreds of miles to become a savage. Being a savage is the mental belief in yourself and your greatness. Find a way that you can dig deeper to discover what pushes you forward and tie that into your mental fortitude to build a strong belief in yourself. It is not the success at the end that defines you, but the journey itself and the grit you use along the way.

David didn't find the success he is famous for by accomplishing his goals on the first try. No, he failed multiple times until failure was neutralized. His belief was so strong that he simply learned from his failures and set about the task again, never willing to give up. Those hard goals we set for ourselves are ways that we can bring out the very best versions of ourselves, and that is what the world needs.

Savage lessons

1. Being a real leader means uplifting your team.
2. Failure is a part of the process, but picking yourself up after failing is what sets you apart from the rest of the crowd.
3. Build belief in yourself—the most important lesson.

Ultimate Goal

1. Set yourself one big goal that will take all your grit to reach. Write it down and stare at it each day.

Final Action Step

Be the person who leads by example through grit and determination, not to prove you are better than others, but to uplift them and help push them to reach beyond their perceived limits. Show them what it means to be a true leader and then challenge them to show someone else.

Thank you!

To The Point Publishing is a collective of students, writers, editors, designers, and researchers that strive to create the best summary books and workbooks on the market.

We would like to thank you for helping us support our passions. We hope you learned new and exciting information from this book that will carry on into your daily lives.

If you enjoyed this book, would you please scan the QR code below and leave a five-star review? It will help us to continue to publish books and take care of our collective business.

Made in the USA
Monee, IL
11 September 2023

42556504R00031